Embroidered Truth

Embroidered Truth

By: Patricia Gilmour

GILMOUR PUBLISHING
New Zealand
December 2024
ISBN - 978-1-0670074-9-2

I am both an Artist and Writer

I can call myself both and artist and a writer and am finding I have a lifetime of experiences to draw on.

I used to think that my life was boring and nobody would be interested to read about me.   I no longer believe that to be true. The more I paint and write the more ideas flow out of me. All sorts of stories and situations I have been in. With my writing in particular I often draw on personal life experiences but my writing is not limited to that.

In most instances I write about what I know. I have lived it. Felt the rejection, sadness and loneliness. Felt unimportant, felt that I don't matter, and felt I would not be missed if I was no longer here. The good thing is that I am here, I matter and I have stories to tell. Many many stories…

Being an artist and writer has been an ambition since childhood but was put aside as I felt it was an unreachable goal.

My love of reading was started one Christmas when we were holidaying in Dargaville, Northland, New Zealand, at my grandparents, my mum's parents.

As a Christmas gift I received an Enid Blyton book, Five Run Away Together. My reaction was it was too big and I could not read it.

I remember starting to read this book, lying on a stretcher in one of the bedrooms and I could not put the book down. Any spare moment I got I would be reading.

Reading as a child not only improved my spelling and understanding words beyond my years, but also my vocabulary.

As a young adult one of my co-workers in a jeans factory where I was working objected to the "long" words I was using.

As a child I dreamed of being "discovered" for want of a better word, and becoming famous. Riding my bike down the street and singing. I also liked singing and my favourite music group was ABBA. I had posters of ABBA on my bedroom walls, lots of posters. I was never "discovered"…

I have sold artworks and books, so am an artist and author.

Table of Contents

1. Triangle

I want to share with you my experience of the
Hauraki Triangle. Now the triangle is located in a
section of the Hauraki Gulf, unknown location as it
tends to move around and many have been
unavoidably caught up as a result.

This particular day I had set out with my friends,
Katherine, Peter, Shirley, Wayne and Graham, in
Graham's motor boat, for a fun day out on the
water, which proved to be anything but fun. It was
a sunny summer's day with not a cloud in the sky
but that was to quickly change.

Very soon we noticed dark stormy clouds
appearing swiftly on the horizon. It happened so
fast. We could do nothing. No time to return to
shore. To safety.

We were buffeted, back and forth between the
waves. All we could do was hang on for our lives.
Yes we had heard the stories. Most people
believed they were urban myths. Stories told
around the campfire. We were soon to learn they
were all true.

Just as quickly as the storm started it was over and we found ourselves afloat our vessel in this beautiful blue lagoon just off from this sandy beach that seemed to stretch for miles. Not sure how this could be though. Seemed like an illusion. A mirage if you will. I did wonder if I could be dreaming. But no, I was not dreaming!

We put down the anchor, sorted some basic supplies, erected our small vessel, loaded our supplies and launched the dingy into the water and made our way to what appeared to be a deserted beach.

Appearances can be very deceiving. We were being watched. Once we landed we dragged the dinghy up the sand so it would not be dragged out by the tide. Then we went to explore.

It was so quiet and tranquil. On each of our minds was that we should find or build some form of shelter. Something to protect us from the elements should the weather suddenly turn bad again.

What happened next would only make the mind boggle in disbelief. Suddenly we were surrounded. We had noticed signs that there were others on this island so had been proceeding quietly and carefully as we did not know where we were or how primitive the natives might turn out to be.

I had seen pictures of early Moriori and their native dress, flax woven into coverings. The natives appeared to be Moriori. They spoke in a language similar sounding to Maori. I could pick out a word here and there but nothing that made much sense.

I kept hearing the word kai over and over. This instilled even more fear in us as we realised that we were going to be the kai.

I am rather sketchy as to how we managed to escape the natives, but escape we did. There was some sort of commotion. To me it sounded more like an explosion.

This seemed to frighten the natives and they dispersed rather hastily and so before they could make a reappearance we took off back to the boat, dragging our dinghy back to the water and rowing as fast as we could to get away from these primitive natives. We did not want to become their next meal.

Just as suddenly as earlier we noticed storm clouds fast approaching and again we were buffeted, back and forth between the waves.

This time it was different in that after the storm, one by one we each awoke, still aboard our vessel.

The whole experience seemed to be a dream, as if we had each fallen asleep in the sun.

The thing was that when we discussed our experience, each one of us had, had the same "dream".

It is for you to decide if my story actually happened or if we, a group of six friends decided to make up yet another urban myth.

2. Early Life

Life has not been easy for me and I have had many personal challenges, though mixed in with the challenges have also been good times so generally life has been good.

I became a Christian as a teenager which had a huge impact on how I came to view my life, morals and ethics. I was a lot happier during this time, I made friends.

Prior to this time I was quite lonely. Even though technically I was not an only child I grew up like one as I was the only one still living at home with my parents by the age of 7. I became an aunty around that time as my 3 siblings are so much older than I am, 10 plus years.

As a result my childhood was rather lonely. My parents worked full time, until mum had a stroke when I was about 15.

My parents had their own interests, so were often not home. I felt their hobbies were more important than I was. They went away every year to the indoor bowling nationals. I usually stayed at my sister Lyn's place.

I spent half my time at Lyn's and it was twice the distance to Peachgrove Intermediate where I attended so I needed to leave extra early on my bike to get to school on time.

I had no choice what high school I went to, was in the zone for Hamilton Girl's High. Looking back that was a blessing as I could have gotten in with the wrong crowd and my life choices could have been very different.

If I had attended a co-ed school I could have been very negatively influenced. There was one such school close to where Lyn lived but due to zoning I could not go there.

Becoming a Christian, at age 15, largely due to joining ISCF, Interschool Christian Fellowship, guided me into making good choices with my life.

Walking to catch the bus home from school I generally had my nose in a book, not the safest thing to do. Would read on the bus, walking down the road, between classes. Always had a book with me. I also became a school librarian helping out during lunch time and if not rostered on would still hang out there.

When I became a Christian and started attending church regularly, Fairfield Presbyterian Church, going to Bible Class on Sunday evenings, I came across the poem on the following page in a magazine:

a. **The Four Calls**

The Spirit came in childhood and pleaded, "Let me
in"
But oh! The door was bolted, by thoughtlessness
and sin
"I am too young" the child replied, "I will not
yield today
There's time enough tomorrow", the Spirit went
away.

Again He came and pleaded, in youth's bright
happy hour;
He came but heard no answer, for lured by Satan's
power
The Youth lay dreaming then, and saying "Not
today,
Nor till I've tried earth's pleasures" The Spirit
went away.

Again he called in mercy, in manhood's vigorous
prime
But still he found no welcome, the Merchant had
no time
No time for true repentance, no time to think or
pray
And so repulsed and saddened, the Spirit went
away

Once more he called and waited, the man was old
and ill
He scarcely heard the whisper, his heart was cold
and still
"Go leave me; when I need thee, I'll call for thee"
he cried
Then sinking on his pillow, without a hope he
died.

Author Unknown

I was a new Christian in 1980 when I first read this
poem. We did not have the internet back then.
We read the newspaper and magazines. Google is
wonderful, as what I could not recall I was able to
fill in the gaps. There are also different versions of
this poem. It was published in 1951 or even earlier
and at some stage it was put to music and printed
in 7 hymnals. I feel this poem is timeless and still
has meaning and impact in today's world.

b. **Rosemary Taniwha**

When I was a child my best friend was Rosemary Taniwha, a Maori girl a little older than I was. I lived at 1 Riwi Street, Te Awamutu and Rosemary was at number 5.

Rosemary's house was older and the toilet was a small shed down a path with a pull down chain to flush.   The bathroom was in the house. In my house the toilet was in the wash house that was attached to the house off the back porch.

I remember a holiday where I went with Rosemary's family to their batch. We tried to walk to the sea but it was too far. I also crawled through brush. Great memories. It must have been Easter as I recall receiving an Easter egg, chicken in a cup.

I also recall going with Rosemary and her family eel fishing. We were positioned along a river. I did not catch any eels. Eel fishing was not very exciting, sitting there waiting for something to happen.

My parents and I moved to Hamilton and
Rosemary and I drifted apart, though she did come
for a couple of holidays. We went to Claudlands
Bush one day and Rosemary cleaned an area of the
bush with a makeshift broom to create a
house. Next time I went to Claudlands Bush I
could not find it as leaves had covered the area
over.

I often went to my sister Lyn's in the school
holidays. Lyn was married with a baby. Mum
worked so could not look after me during the
school holidays.

In Hamilton I became friends with Debbie who
lived over the road. On the way to Lyn's we called
in to Rosemary's house. Debbie thought we were
staying there so got out her suitcase. She had to be
told to put it back in the car, we were just visiting.

After that time I lost contact with
Rosemary. Rosemary's family moved away and I
did not know where to. Through the years I
wanted to find Rosemary. She was my best friend,
even though I had made other friends I never
forgot her.

With the internet I did searches to try to locate her. I tried Facebook when Facebook became popular. Most people are on Facebook.

One day I came across someone with the last name of Taniwha. I had not come across anyone with that last name up until that point. I asked if she was related to Rosemary.

I remembered Rosemary had a younger brother by the name of Thomas. I was put in contact with Thomas and we chatted on messenger. Thomas told me a bit about her life and that she had died about 10 years previously. To this day I am sad that we never got the chance to reconnect.

c.   **Cheryl Paikau**

A friend I made when we moved to Fairfield, a
suburb of Hamilton was Cheryl Paikau. We
became friends at primary school in the early
1970's.

Because of Cheryl I went for a while to Sunday
school at the Salvation Army church close to her
house.

I also tagged along to Every Girl's Rally. I don't
think she was too keen on my attendance as I kinda
invited myself. Transport was provided and I was
picked up from my home in the suburb of Fairfield
in Hamilton.

I did not know much about the Bible, that Jesus
was on the cross between two sinners. I learnt this
from Cheryl when she made plastercine crosses
and put them on the wall in the small back room in
my house. The room I alternated as a playroom
and my bedroom.

I also learnt how to spell the word people. She
wrote the word people, also at my house. We were

playing in the garden shed at the time. It is
amazing what one recalls from childhood.

Dad can't have been home when she was over as
my friends were afraid of my dad. I don't know
why. I was not scared of my dad. He grumbled a
lot but that was just my dad.

Spose those who did not know him well he came
across as scary. My dad really did not bite. Dad
was a gentle man. My pets loved him. My dog
Sandy, a golden lab, in particular loved him. Dad
would call her silly moo and the like and she
would just wag her tail.

At primary school Cheryl got ulcers in her
mouth. Not sure what causes ulcers in the mouth
but Cheryl got them.

Cheryl was also a bit accident prone. At school one
day she knocked her elbow and had to go to sick
bay. She often did things without thinking.

Looking back that would have been why she had that freak accident. The one that ended her life.

Cheryl and I with a couple of other friends held a stall a couple of times at primary school selling sweets, homemade fudge and gave the proceeds to the school.

Somehow I became the leader of the fundraising stall and was in charge. I am not a natural leader so not sure how that happened.

We were in the same class when we got to Intermediate school and Cheryl was my cooking partner in home economics.

That year I made a couple of other friends, Linda and Jeanette, so I did not spend as much time hanging out with Cheryl. I really regret that as in the August school holidays Cheryl had that freak accident and was killed.

Cheryl had gone with her family to a country fair. While her sister was on the mini ferris wheel, Cheryl ran up calling to her sister and put her head between two bars. She was killed instantly.

I have never forgotten my friend. I never have and never will forget Cheryl. I believe I will see her one day in heaven. I did not go to her funeral as my mother advised me to stay away. I do wish I had gone to her funeral, to say goodbye properly.

Cheryl was Maori so her funeral would have been called a tangi and knowing what I do now of the Maori way of doing things I would have been welcome to attend. I would have been treated as whanau.

d. **ISCF**

When I was at high school I started attending ISCF (Inter School Christian Fellowship) at lunch time. It was held in the music room. We would eat our lunch together, sing from a Songs of Praise booklet. I enjoyed singing.

The teachers that ran it were Mrs Gordon and Mrs Curran. Mrs Gordon taught English but I was not in any of her classes and Mrs Gordon was my biology teacher.

I felt I was not a popular kid and was quite lonely. I did not have many friends.

One Saturday there was a combined event with another school. I attended. There was a question we were asked. *"One thing I wanted in life and to write it down".* My thing was to be liked.

Mrs Gordon's response to that was *"but I do like you".* That one sentence has meant so much to me through the years and has helped me through some struggling times. That's what I needed at that time in my life. That someone liked me and cared enough to say so.

Teachers can have a real impact on students both positive and negative. Both Mrs Gordon and Mrs Curran were positive influences in my life.

Another influence Mrs Gordon had on me was that she told me that a Christian should never be afraid to apologise.

I had had an argument with my mother one morning before coming to school and had told Mrs Gordon about it.

I went home that afternoon and apologised to my mother. She did not actually hear the apology as she had fallen asleep in her chair.

The important thing was that I had apologised. I learnt a valuable lesson that day. It is okay to admit to myself and others when I am in the wrong and to do something about it. Never let pride stand in your way.

I have also learnt to apologise when I am not in the wrong in order to maintain friendships. Sadly this is not how I have often been treated by both family and friends.

Forgiveness is important. Moreso for the person needing to forgive than the person being forgiven but I do find that the trust is often gone if the person I have needed to forgive has not apologised and acknowledged their wrong doing.

Even years later it can affect me and it is even worse when it is perhaps a church leader or someone in ministry that really should know better. *That is that hard thing, they should know better and be humble enough to admit when they have made a mistake.*

e. **Childhood
Recollections**

My first banking experience was with the Post
Office Savings Bank. Schools in those days
organised for every child to have a savings account
and we were encouraged to bring in our bank
account book with a little money each week to
save.

When my grandfather's estate was wound up I
received a small inheritance, less than $100, I
thought I was rich.

The cheque was deposited into my savings
account. This was the very first cheque that had
my name on it. It came from a solicitor. I was not
expecting anything.

Afterall Grandad died when I was 3 so I hardly
remembered him. I only have a small recollection
of him and I am not sure how reliable that is or if it
was something I have been told.

Childhood recollections may not be that
accurate. I also recall I fell out of a moving car
when I was 3 and for years after the event I have a
recollection of getting up and running after the
car.

No one confirmed if this actually happened so
even I am doubtful. It was a small car and was
referred to as a bomb.

That is an old beaten up vehicle. This was in the
60's. No seatbelts in those days. I had leaned on
the car door and it had flown open.

Since then I have been careful about car doors and
never lean on them. It was not our family car, if
we had one, but a car belonging to a family that
often looked after me as both my parents worked.

The Snowden family lived on top of a hill next to a
bush in Te Kuiti where I was born. I started school
in Te Kuiti. I was taken somewhere to be checked
out to make sure I was fine. I was.

My first recollection of our family car was the car that Dad brought home, either just before or just after Grandad had died. It was a grey Humber Hawke and came with an operating manual, as they did back then, complete with diagrams. This meant Dad was able to fix any issues and it did not need to go into a garage.

When I was shopping for my first car I was discouraged from getting an automatic for this very reason, as he or my brother John would not be able to fix it for me, it would have to go into a garage for any maintenance needing to be done.

3.   **My Nana Rhodes** – A Child's story – dealing with grief.

My name is Samantha but shortened to Sam, except when I have been naughty, then I am called Samantha. Whenever we were in Auckland we had to visit an old lady. My Aunty Mavis said. Aunty Mavis did not mind if we did not go see her, though often we did.

Aunty Mavis lived in a place that sounded like Tallbay. I liked the views from the windows in her house. It looked out over the sea. I liked looking at the sea.

I did not like the place with the old people. It was dingy and smelt funny. Chairs were lined against the walls with old people in them. Lots of old people. They all looked sad.

Aunty Mavis said we had to go see Nana Rhodes. She was old and one day she would die and we would never see her again. This made me sad. Then she did die. I was sad.

Everyone went to what was called a funeral. I did not go. I was told I was too young to go. A while after Nana Rhodes died I got a letter with a piece of paper that I was told was money and to put in

my bank account. I had one of those. The money
paper was from Grandad Rhodes who had died
before Nana Rhodes.

I was three years old when Grandad Rhodes died
so do not remember much about him. I think
Grandad Rhodes had a black beard. Grandad lay
down in the shed one morning and just did not
wake up again. Nana Rhodes went looking for
him as he had not come in for breakfast. This was
sad. I was told it was ok to be sad.

*I wrote the above story drawing from my own
personal experience with my Nana Gilmour when
as child of about 10. I have used this story and
developed it into a children's picture book and
called it "My Nana Rhodes".*

4.   Bird Cage

Hello, my name is Megan and on this particular day I decided to clean my bird cage that my dad had made for my budgies out of an old wooden television set. Dad even made a metal pull out tray for the bottom of the cage to make it easy to clean.

In later years I realised just how special my dad was and by making me that bird cage was his way of showing how much he cared.

Dad was never one to show affection by hugging but by doing practical things for me. Creating a bird cage was very practical and looking back it was made out of love.

Back to this one particular day when I decided to "clean" the cage. I got out the vacuum cleaner. Back in the 1970's in most households there would be an Electrolux vacuum cleaner.

I found cleaning out the cage with a vacuum cleaner was a very poorly thought out idea. One lives and learns and does not repeat one's mistakes. Well, we hope mistakes do not get repeated. A mistake it was!

You see, one of my budgies, who I had named Luke, on account of his colour. He was a lutino, decided at that very moment to fly low and almost got vacuumed up by the cleaner.

How he survived I will just never know, as it does not take much for a bird to die of fright.

It is often when someone special, in this instance my dad, is no longer with us that we realise just how precious they are and what a great hole they have left in our lives that we fully appreciate who they were.

I wrote the story above and is based on a childhood experience.

5.   Horses and Ponies

In my 20's I got involved with horses, by this time
I was living in Rotorua and had the opportunity to
do a horsecare scheme. I always liked horses but
as a child I did not have the opportunity to be
around them very often.

Doing the horsecare scheme I learnt the basics of
how to care for a horse, grooming, leading,
saddling up though not so much the riding side of
things.

From there I moved to Matamata and worked in a
top New Zealand racing stable as one of the
ground crew. It was long hours, 4.30 in the
morning start and only one full day off every
second week (Sunday).

I found I had no life outside of work so gave in my
notice after 7 months and moved to South
Auckland where my brother and his family lived. I
went to stay with them for a while.

My love for horses remained. I quickly found
employment working at the Wholesale Tree
Company, Airfield Road, Takanini.

I would catch the train from Papatoetoe and get off at the Takanini train station and walk to work past the training track and would see all these horses being ridden back from the track and this made me nostalgic every day.

This was until I got my driver's licence and purchased my first car.

Then I was given a thoroughbred straight of the track. Bruiser had just retired from racing when he retired from racing. I had looked after him on the horsecare scheme.

Bruiser and I were not a good combination. I was a learner rider. It was ok during winter and I gained confidence riding along the road. He was good in traffic apart from motorbikes. The problems really started when spring arrived. Spring grass!

I had horsey friends and so took him along to
Takanini Pony Club. Well, in hindsight, knowing
what I know now, he probably thought he was at
the races with all the other horses. He turned into
a bucking bronco.

It was amazing I did not come off him and was not
seriously hurt. The pony club was next to Totara
Park where there was a bridle path. That was
another time he got difficult.

We went to our first ribbon day held, by an adult
riding group, The Sore Butt Club, as they called
themselves.

This ribbon day was held at Manurewa Pony Club.
One of the members picked us up in her float.
Well Bruiser was difficult on this day as well and
was hard to handle. Again he probably thought he
was at the races. I learnt I was overhorsed.

I should never been given Bruiser. The trainer,
from the horsecare scheme, who gave him to me
knew my lack of ridden experience. Bruiser
needed a very experienced rider. I sold him on to
someone much better able to handle him.

I looked for another horse. I put up a wanted advertisement in a local horsegear store and I received a phone call about Miles coming available.   A Standardbred gelding. Much more suitable.

So many great memories I had with Miles and he was my riding horse for the next 6 years.

While I was trialling him I took him on a Sore Butt trek and he was great. We did countless fun ribbon days.

There were four pony clubs within riding distance, Takanini Pony Club, Manurewa Pony Club, Papatoetoe Pony Club and Pointways Pony Club.

Only Pointways Pony Club is still going today, though Papatoetoe Pony Club relocated to new grounds.

Takanini Pony Club and Botany Pony Club combined and became Totara Park Riding Club at the other end of Totara Park as the council did not want a pony club at both ends of Totara Park.

a. **Milestone Ace**

I went for miles and miles on Milestone Ace
Red meant stop, green for go
Traffic backing up, not enough metal
I very soon realised, to trigger the light.

It is only a little jump, the judge said
So we chanted over and over, "is only a little jump
When we got there, Miles and I were both
convinced
And sailed over "the little jump."

Over motorway bridges, took our chances with
traffic
No shying ever, did not want to go splat
Fall down on the motorway, to stop traffic and
cause accidents
He was so safe was Milestone Ace.

Miles had personality, he could let me know his
disgust with one look
If he had not seen me for a bit, had missed me
Though he soon forgave, Miles loved me
Carrots usually did the trick.

Get a fright, check for traffic
Trot across the road, to finish his fright
One in a million horse, I once was told
Was Milestone Ace.

b. **Ridgeway Shamrock**

Ridgeway Shamrock was a very special pony. A full Connemara pony which is a breed that originated from Ireland, a place called Connemara.

I called Shamrock Sham or Shammy mostly and she was a part of my life for more than 18 years and gave me many great memories. I lost her at the age of 32. The day I found her down in the paddock and waiting for the vet to arrive I was able to thank Shammy for all the great memories and for being my friend.

Shammy had her quirks, like most ponies. The one thing she did not like were vehicles backfiring. Probably cause it sounded like a gunshot. She would leap in the air and move sideways, this happened one day being ridden in the paddock.

I found with Shammy the better I rode the better she went. One day my teenage niece Tracy decided she wanted to have a ride.

Tracy rode off and a few minutes later came back in disgust. Tracy was not able to get Shammy to canter. Sham would have been sussing out if this kid could ride. Tracy was not a beginner and had her own horse. That was Sham.

Sham also did not like just anyone riding her. I once told a friend, Kristine, this when she wanted to ride Sham.

Kristine got on and Shammy threw her head up and squealed. Kristine then understood.

Prior to me owning Shammy, she had done RDA work, even been used in a display, ridden with no gear on, in a demonstration for Princess Anne and was at a trekking place, so she definitely preferred one main rider. I was that rider.

I had lost my confidence prior to finding Shammy. Shammy got my confidence back. The day I met her, I walked, trotted and cantered her in the paddock and she did not bolt. I took her.

Shammy was the most I have ever paid for any horse or pony but was well worth it.

When I got Shammy back to pony club I had not
cantered again before our first ribbon day. We got
a first equal ribbon.

My favourite event at ribbon days was look alike
horse and rider. We did really well in that event. It
would have been judged on suitability of horse and
rider, working as a good combination.

Shammy had a slow trot but was free moving at
the canter, it was also a controlled canter. We also
jumped small jumps, having to do circles before
the jump. Very amusing to watch. I have it on
video. Shammy was a very safe pony and I will
miss her always.

c. **Miniature Horses**

In the early 2000's I met Amanda. Amanda contacted me over an item I was selling on TradeMe. She said "I have miniature horses, come and have a look". This was my introduction to the mini horse.

At the time Amanda had a couple of horses for sale. I kept telling her I had no money, but ended up agreeing to buy Smudge from her, a chestnut and white pinto.

The item I was selling on TradeMe became my deposit and I paid off the balance over the coming weeks.

Amanda is one of my closest friends to this day. She also got me Betsy as a yearling, we were part owners for some time. I still have Betsy. Her foaling date is 16 September 2002.

Betsy has had 5 babies, all colts. One of them is doing well in a riding school in French Polynesia.

Smooch was sold as a 4 year old about 9 years ago. Smooch's younger brother Tomeo was a foal at the time. Sadly I lost Tomeo at the age of 7 due to a rare case of colic.

d. **Home Invasion**

Unloading groceries from the car
One less loaf of bread

Ran off with it
With witnesses
Merry the accused

Non impressed neighbour
Twas her loaf of bread
Funny side seen by me
Her not so much
Only a loaf of bread

Merry with Pippin,
Partner in crime
What a mess was made
Into the flour, sugar, macaroni too
Scone mixture on the floor

Lovely time was had
Me not so much

Took days to clean
The "lovely" mess

As was mixed in with water
From the dog bowl on the floor

I wrote the poem "Home Invasion" about two naughty minis.

I still have Merry. Pippin was sold to become a small child's pet, riding pony.

I had stopped harness driving Pippin as there were times he would play up in the cart, one such time was at Scurry Fun where he bolted, bucked as he changed direction realising we were about to crash into a parked vehicle.

As he bucked and changed direction I was turfed out of the cart so felt I could not drive him after that.

Pippin has always been great with kids so felt he needed a career change.

6.   Anthology – Tales from Dominion Road

On Facebook I joined an Auckland writers group – I have included my written submissions I specially wrote for the anthology, though only a poem and painting were accepted.

A bit of background – my first job was in a knitwear factory at 330 Dominion Road, Mt Eden, Auckland.

I worked there for 2 years so based my writing from that experience with a bit of exaggeration for effect.

a. **Creeping Roses**

Dominion Road is a long road in Mt Eden, Auckland. It was my first place of employment, in a knitwear factory. I got to know the area quite well in the early 1980s.

All the factory workers finished at 3 pm on Friday afternoons and for a while I got quite nostalgic as I headed back to the Baptist Youth Hostel, in Gillies Avenue, Epsom, a neighbouring suburb, where I lived for that first year away from all I knew to be familiar.

I had moved to Auckland from Hamilton, a much smaller city. Early finishing on Friday afternoons, school was out. Kids on their way home.

That had been my life up until recently. I rode a push bike to work, downhill to work, uphill back to the hostel where I was living for that first year.

It was easier to walk up the hills. There was this creepy old guy in his garden that would talk to me and ask personal things like "Do you have a boyfriend?" "Was I a virgin?" Such inappropriate questions for anyone, but especially an old guy to be asking a 16 year old such things.

I was a friendly person and in some ways a little too trusting and had led a relatively sheltered life.

Even in my naivety I sensed the potential danger. He scared me and I was not exactly sure why. He had not done anything physically inappropriate, just his questions. He had not tried to grab me but then it was just after 3 pm in the afternoon and there were people around to come to my aid.

One Friday afternoon he offered to show me his roses and for me to come around the side of the house.   "Stay away from me" I shouted as I got on my bike and as quickly as I could I peddled away, desperately hoping he would not have the energy to chase me.

This day the street appeared deserted. As I got to the top of the hill I looked back and he was still standing in his garden.

After that day I went a different way back to the Hostel, which was longer but much safer.

I never told anyone of this experience. I should have, as I may not necessarily have been the only young girl this creepy old guy entered into

conversation with, asking questions he had no right
to ask.

He could have been harmless. I certainly hope he
was, though that is doubtful considering the things
he asked and that nothing bad happened to another
naive girl on her way past.

b. Serving Time at Reno Fashions

Well what can I say!
My lag was for 1 year 11 months
Day in, day out – Monday to Friday

Mundane stripping
Mundane cleaning
Mundane beverage making

Washing dishes.

Thought I had disproved
One does not need an education
Qualifications
To get a job

I walked into this job
Or so it seemed

Was a dead end job though
Going nowhere

Stay at school
Get an education
Do a course
Apprenticeship

Something

Opens opportunities
Sets one up for life

Not so mundane
As being a professional stripper.

c. **Bell Control**

The bell rings. One thinks that by leaving school that there will be no more bells.

Not true. The alarm clock wakes one up to get up and get ready for work.

My dad was my alarm clock when I was still living at home and going to school. He would wake me at 7 am and tell me it was time to get up, to get ready for school.

There can be bells to tell you when you can take your morning, lunch and afternoon tea breaks.

There is also the clocking in and out or signing a timesheet or card.

The final bell for the day is when it is time to go home. This is a form of control. All in order to earn a "living."

The building of 330 Dominion Road, Mt Eden has been used for several businesses over the years including Greenstone Pictures Limited. Back in the early 1980's it was Reno Fashions which was a knitwear factory.

My first job after leaving school at age 16. Back then I was not academically minded, or so I thought. This was my life for the next two years.

My first day of work was the Tuesday after Anniversary Weekend. I relocated to Auckland from my hometown of Hamilton to take the job. It was a big step. An exciting step. And it happened really fast. All in the space of a week.

The factory front looks very different now. In the front of the building there was a shoe shop. I bought a pair of gold sandals that only survived one wearing.

There was also an op shop. In fact the whole area looks so different. I was such a quiet person way back then, had low confidence to such a degree that there was one lady, Margaret, who bullied me.

It got really bad, the way Margaret bossed me around and spoke to me, quite nastily.

This was noticed by all the other factory workers. The behaviour went on for quite some time.

I had been used to being bullied at school so thought it was "normal" to be treated in this fashion.

The other factory staff did not like what they saw and realised the unfairness of it. They intervened. Margaret was a very hard working Maori lady

Margaret was made to stop. Not sure if it was a racial issue that caused her to treat me that way or simply an unwarranted dislike of me. Or I was just picked on cause she "could".

It was a multicultural workforce, the bosses were Yugoslavian. It was a family business. Two brothers and their mother worked there as a cutter.

One of my work mates was a young girl from Rarotonga - Raro as she called it.

From what she told me. I now would think that she was possibly in an abusive relationship. Her last name was a repeat of her first name, so she told me, though being so long ago I do not recall with certainty what it was.

How I came to work at Reno Fashions was that I had just left school and my sister Lyn got me an interview at another factory on Dominion Road.

I did not know Auckland at all so Lyn came with me to the interview and then we heard of another factory so went and asked if they had any position openings.

In the early 1980's it was easy to get a job in a factory when one has little or no experience and this is what happened. The position would be kept open for me but I needed to find a closer place to live as commuting from my brother John's place in Manurewa was not an option.

They did not want to train me and then have me leave as I could not cope with the daily commute.

I started the following week after I had moved and settled into the Baptist Youth Hostel in Gillies Avenue, Epsom.

A new friend I made at the hostel, Cheryl, came with me over that Anniversary Weekend and we walked to Dominion Road to see how long it would take. It took 40 minutes.

We decided this was quite manageable as a start. The first few days I walked to work until John got me a pushbike. Was all downhill so the journey took much less time getting to work that first year, longer getting back to the hostel.

I did a variety of different tasks in this factory - some machine operation but that was minor. They were supposed to train me but that never actually eventuated.

I started helping the tea lady who also was the packer and then she got ill and I took over looking after the lunchroom and the necessary cleaning.

I was called into the office one day and asked if I would clean the staff and management toilets and by doing so I would find an extra $5 in my pay packet each week.

It was on the understanding that I would keep this between myself and management. Being a naive 16 year old I did as I was told. Not sure if any laws were being broken here.

My main task though, was as a professional stripper. In the process of construction of knitwear garments there is a process that was referred to as stripping.

This is the removal of some rows of yarn around the neckline of the garment after the neckline was attached. I did so much of it that I even dreamed of stripping. The work was repetitive.

There was also a sock division downstairs and I worked down there for a while amongst all the noise of the industrial knitting machines.

So many breaches of health and safety back in the 1980's as no earmuffs were provided. This would not happen now. It was a different time and people were not so politically correct.

Even in the main factory it was very noisy, radios blaring over the work noise. Definitely so much quieter in the lunchroom where I also worked preparing everyone's hot drinks and clearing up afterwards.

It was tradition that on your birthday, the birthday person would buy a selection of cakes for all the factory workers morning tea.

When my time came around I took my turn. What I had not realised was that I would be presented with a "huge" bouquet of flowers.

I was living away from where I grew up, my first job, all that was familiar. My work colleagues recognised this and wanted to make the day special for me. It was such a lovely gesture and completely unexpected.

Made me feel special as I had left my friends in Hamilton in such a hurry and had not had a chance to say goodbye to my church group and have a proper send off.

I think that is what affected me the most, not saying bye to my friends. My church group did, however, send me a card wishing me well on my venture.

I was able to catch up from time to time when I went home to Hamilton on weekends.

I made new friends in Auckland at the hostel and made new friends at my new church, Epsom Baptist Church.

7.   Adult Learning and Employment

I went back to high school as an adult student, much to the amusement of my nieces.

I was at the time living in a flat at the back of my brother John's property.

It had come to the point in my life that I had moved from one dead end job to another and at that time in my life I was taking some time out to find out what I wanted to do career wise with my life.

I was busy, while unemployed. I used to joke that if I had a job where would I fit it in. I had my horse, Miles, undertook voluntary work from time to time and was involved at the local Baptist church – Papatoetoe Baptist. My life was anything but mundane.

I had felt under pressure and was being judged by another branch of the family. I also did not feel I needed to justify my actions and decisions to them. They were not me. I needed that time and when the time was right I did something about it.

My first step was to go back to high school. Manurewa High School gave me that opportunity.

I took School Certificate English, History and Six Form Film Studies. The students in my history and English classes accepted me but not so much the students in my film studies class.

They were a bit snobby and standoffish. That year I passed School Certificate and Film Studies and narrowly missed out passing History.

I had taken history when I was originally at high school and the curriculum was similar. I found it interesting.

Being an adult student I was far better equipped and was able to apply myself so much than when I was younger.

The interesting thing was my third form teacher and English teacher at Hamilton Girl's High, Mrs Pinkney, was now teaching Japanese at Manurewa High School. Mrs Pinkney recognised me and we had a catch up.

The following year I had the opportunity of doing a tech course with the Manukau Institute of

Technology, Papakura Campus, Introduction to Office Skills.

This course covered a wide variety of subjects, typewriting where I gained Pitman's Advanced.

I had taking typing at high school. I have never been a fast typist. It was the day before the exam that I was given the opportunity of doing Pitman's Advanced Typewriting.

There was a spare space and it was offered to two of us, we were basically top of the class, the other girl declined. What my tutor said I lacked in speed I made up for in knowledge. I passed.

The course was wonderful and I had great tutors I learnt a lot from them. However, I did have issues with a couple of the other adult students who were rather hurtful.

We had an exercise where we had to find pictures in a magazine and cut them out. One of the other students brought a picture back into the classroom, where I was working on the project, a picture of someone with their mouth zipped up and gave it to me.

Yes I do talk a lot, yes I do have a lot to say sometimes but that is no excuse for meanness.

That is what it was. I was crushed. The two mean students were ones that were struggling in the class.

I was at the top, though they had no issue with the other girl who was also at the top of the class. Just me.

Yet that particular student, a mature student, had spoken previously about being sensitive and being hurt easily.

Now I am sensitive and hurt very easily. Someone who experiences rejection easily does not intentionally inflict the same onto others and that is what she did to me that day.

The interesting thing I found after I graduated from the course, Introduction to Office Skills, was that I had all these certificates saying I could do all these wonderful things but every job I applied for wanted someone with experience. No one would give me a chance. Except for Mr Sanders!

a. **Law Office**

I did some cold calling on the phone looking for work. One of the calls I made was to a lawyer, John Sanders, who said his office person was leaving, was not sure when as she had a house she was selling and was going back to the UK.

About three week later Mr Sanders called me to come in for some training. I was to take over her position when she left. Initially it was going to be for two hours a day which was fine as the law office was a short walk from my flat in Old Papatoetoe. It was quicker to walk than drive and look for parking.

This was my introduction to trust accounting. Trust accounting is a specialised field and everything has to be exact and cannot even be a cent out as it is managing client funds.

If any errors are made it needs to be well documented. Law Society inspectors come and do random audits from time to time and so long as any discrepancy can be explained, that it has been rectified immediately, there is usually no issue.

I found I really enjoyed accounts work, playing with money. My official title was accounts clerk.

I owe a lot to John Sanders for giving me this opportunity to prove myself. He was a strange man in some ways.

And you see, when I did get a job I did manage to fit it all in. This job quickly became almost full time. I asked for my own key as often I would be outside waiting for Mr Sanders to arrive and let me in when I could have already been working.

My colleague, Marie, the word processing operator, one day when I arrived to work told Mr Sanders I was not an octopus. That was when Mr Sanders was bombarding me with things he needed. I had not even taken off my coat.

Mr Sanders was near retirement age when I started working for him and one day he decided he was going to learn to type so borrowed Marie's typewriter.

He had a friend with him in his office and he attempted to type out a letter for her. The friend brought it out and asked if Marie or I could redo it.

I took the letter and retyped it for her. The letter had no presentation to it whatsoever. It was impressive that someone of Mr Sander's age wanted to learn a new skill.

I gained so much confidence, knowledge and experience working for Mr Sanders that I will forever be grateful.

When work got quieter and my hours dropped right back I launched a small admin business working from home and Mr Sanders became my first client until I was able to train Marie to take over the trust accounting side of things.

My admin business did not go very well as I was not able to secure enough clients who needed their accounts kept up to date.

However, what brought in the money was typing up people's curriculum vitae's. I would do this while they were with me.

The average CV would take an hour to do though a basic one could be done in half an hour.

There was this one guy that his CV took about three hours and he kept changing things, wasting paper and printer ink as this would be after I had printed it out that he made the changes. I was not charging him any extra but he still quibbled about the cost.

This guy was a Christian and single, so he said, and had done missionary work. He went away and came back with flowers.

I could see the funny side though impressing me he was not. I would have preferred the money. He did come back for me to redo his CV at a later date and complained he should not have to pay again. There are some really strange people in this world.

b. **Engineers Printing and Manufacturing Union**

As my admin business was not doing very well I started looking for alternative work and did some temping work in the meantime.

I worked for the Engineer, Printing and Manufacturing Union in Papatoetoe for a few months filling in while the girl who worked there was off on maternity leave as it was called back then.

I was at reception and looked after the Union Organisers. They were great to work with and I did meet Andrew Little, who was at that time the National Secretary for the Engineers Union, later to become a politician and become the leader of the Labour Party.

Head office was in Grafton but there were times when Andrew Little would be in Papatoetoe for meetings which is how I came to meet him.

Towards the end of my temping contract my mother ended up in hospital in a coma with a brain haemorrhage and we were waiting for her to die.

The organisers were great, very supportive. I
would endeavour to do my bit to help them out but
was not there much in my last week as was going
up to Auckland Hospital each day.

One of the organisers even gave me a lift in as he
was going in to head office in Grafton that day.

c. **Birthday Death**

"You know she is going to die, don't you?"
"What a cruel thing to say! I don't need to hear
that right now, leave me alone".
"Hey, don't make a scene!"
"My mother is in a coma and you are not helping".
We had gathered in the whanau room waiting for a
doctor to come and explain to us what was
happening and our options.

Present were other members of the family, my
brother and sister in law, my sister and my other
sister that Paul was married to, their daughter who
I ignored. Perhaps it was the shock. She had done
some injury to herself and was on crutches. She
had been a rather accident prone kid. She
belonged to "that" branch of the family. It was not

in my nature to be unfriendly unless pushed. I was over all the drama.

I had been hearing for years about what that particular branch of the family had been doing and the issues that had been caused. We all knew that Paul was behind it all, controlling my sister Iris.

Convincing our parents to surrender their inheritance early and that they would care for them as they got older. This did not happen. Dad had died 8 years previously. Just mum left now. They had gotten what they wanted. There was nothing left for the rest of us. They had even helped themselves to the family heirlooms that were supposed to go to the oldest son, my brother. It was tradition. They had the opportunity.

I know mum was dying. I just did not want or need it to be so brutally expressed.

The door opened and in walked the doctor. He explained to us that things were not looking good. I barely took it all in. The most they could do was to make mum comfortable. They did not, at this stage, know how long she would still be with us but encouraged us to sit with her and talk to her. Due to the circumstances there was no limit on visiting hours.

I felt so alone. Often misunderstood. I was the youngest in the family and did not have a husband or partner to support me. Often I was the odd one out and felt no one took me seriously and often treated me like I was still a child.

Visiting mum in hospital every day was draining, waiting for her to die. Each day dragged into the next. Each day closer to my birthday. I had just gotten home after visiting mum on my birthday when I got the call. Mum had died.

Mum had hung on until after I had left. It was as if she knew what day it was. She had given birth to me at age 36 and died on my 36th birthday.

I wrote this story for a creative writing course I was doing at the time. It is based on true events with some dramatization.

d. **Criminal Law Firm**

Then I was back to looking for something more permanent. Advertised in the New Zealand was a position at a law office in Otahuhu.

I sent my usual application email over the weekend and on Monday I received a phone call. I put off confirming the interview time but as time did clear for me in the afternoon I went in for an interview.

One of the ladies there indicated I was in with a shot due to my experience, seems the other applicant that was interviewed did not have much experience.

I then called in where I used to work in Papatoetoe, to have a catch up with Mr Sanders and Marie, found out that in between leaving the interview and arriving at Mr Sander's office, Ian had already called John Sanders and asked him about me.

I had left my mobile phone in the car so when I returned to my car I discovered I had a missed call. It was Ian and he wanted me to start the next day, for training and handover.

Ian specialised in criminal law. I ended up working for Ian for 5 years. He was a great boss apart from the many times I could cheerfully have shot him when he was being particularly demanding.

Just imagine the headlines – legal secretary shoots criminal lawyer. Ian knew when he had over stepped the mark as then he would start being nice to me. I could see the funny side. Ian was very good to me. The next lawyer I worked with was not so much. She was psycho, but more about that later.

While working for Ian I saw some interesting things, though probably the biggest was when Ian was representing William Bell, the Panmure RSA triple murderer back in 2002.

I spoke to William Bell on the phone on numerous occasions and he could be very charming. This case went down in history for the longest non parole period in New Zealand history, 33 years but was reduced to 30 years as William Bell appealed the decision.

Ian did say that William Bell would not hesitate to kill again. If William Bell had made different choices with his life he could have made anything of himself as he is actually quite intelligent. In preparation for the trial I had typed up draft documents that Ian took in to the prison when meeting with William Bell and William Bell was correcting my typing errors.

Or perhaps he could simply have been deflecting!

It was a real eye opener working for a criminal lawyer and seeing how other people lived. Especially since I had lived quite a sheltered life in many ways.

There was this lovely young girl that was up on drug charges. The only mistake she made was getting involved with the wrong crowd and so was charged through association.

Fortunately Ian and a barrister, Mark, who was assisting in the case managed to get her off. It was quite a big drug case.

I often asked Ian if the person he was representing was guilty. It was not his place to say and he never gave me an answer as everyone is entitled to fair representation.

One day my former boss, Mr Sanders, visited the office where I worked in Otahuhu. It looked weird to have my former and current boss chatting out on the front deck. The office was in an older style house that was long overdue for renovations.

e. Psycho Boss Lawyer

I had moved to the Waikato and for a year and a half and commuted to Otahuhu every day but found my day was getting longer and longer, especially with all the traffic works so I looked for a job closer and I found one at a law firm in Hamilton.

I was lead to believe my predecessor, we shall call her Katy, had left due to a bit of a scandal and for the first year my new boss, we shall call her Cherie, came across as thinking I was wonderful. This was not to last, as I found.

I was back to managing the accounts. I was very good at trust accounting and keeping records.

There was no handover with my predecessor as Cherie, did not want us to cross paths, so it was either sink or swim and I chose to swim.

Fortunately I was somewhat familiar with aspects of the computer program that was used and this greatly helped and I was able to figure out what I did not already know.

As well as doing the accounts I also prepared trust documentation and other legal documents. I was very good at that job.

Cherie then started looking and going out of her way to make my life difficult, trying to make me make mistakes and when that did not happen it made her very angry.

She would go through my work files after hours, copies of my employment contract disappeared from my desk.

One day I took a stress day not knowing that Cherie would not be in the office that day.

I heard from a co-worker and friend, Jeanette, who supported me through this time. Cherie had gone out of her way to where I was living and had seen me outside putting my miniature horses back in the paddock.

I had been inside all day except for putting a couple of my miniature horses on tethers so they could have grass.

Cherie played mind games. Staff meetings usually consisted of telling me off about something that had been resolved the week before.

I came to dread staff meetings. I would have 4 to 5 bad days a week and often left the office in tears and very stressed. It was not the work, it was the boss I was working for.

There was one instance where Cherie had kept Jeannette and me apart all day.

I was in my office working and Jeannette was working in the boardroom. We met by chance in the ladies at lunchtime.

Jeannette told me were having a staff meeting that afternoon. The staff meeting never eventuated. Right on 5 pm I popped my nose into the boardroom and told Jeannette I had locked the filing cabinets.

The previous week we had accidentally locked all the keys in the filing cabinet instead of retaining the final key and spent ages hunting for the spare set.

Eventually we found the spare set of keys. That was what I mean by a resolved situation that had to be discussed at a staff meeting.

Anyway, Jeannette yelled at me "don't talk to me", twice. I was stunned. I went home crushed. It was Friday so it wasn't until Monday I found out what the problem was.

Cherie had gotten Jeannette into such a state. Jeanette had prepared what she was going to say at the staff meeting and then the meeting was cancelled.

Jeannette had been crying all afternoon. Mind games!

What upset Jeannette also was that I had gone home so she was not able to explain to me what had gone on. Here was my friend who did not normally treat me that way.

I had trained Jeanette in doing my job, in particular accounts and trust accounting. Jeannette picked it up really well.

In any business it is not wise to only have one person to do a job. If that person is away sick or has an accident it causes other issues.

The day I took the stress day Jeannette was able to update the accounts program we used, not just be able to access the information required.

As I knew Cherie was trying so hard to make me leave, which I would have, but I needed the income, I warned Jeannette that if she was offered my position to decline it as if she made a mistake Cherie would come down in her like the proverbial ton of bricks.

As I triple checked my work my error rate was very low. This angered Cherie as she was doing all she could to make me stuff up so she would have an excuse to fire me. I was very good at the job so did not mess up at all.

Jeannette was a great support to me and then once I was gone Cherie treated Jeannette far worse. I later found out from my predecessor, Katy, that there was a history of treating staff that way. We were not the first and second. There was a pattern.

Now we know Cherie went looking for something to get me on and eventually she found it. Being a lawyer she was able to twist things to her own advantage.

Cherie's support person was another lawyer so I had no chance and she even got my support person on side.

Confidentiality; One of my jobs was to open the mail, check emails, print and file appropriately, pay the accounts, put correspondence on client files.

If something came in that it was my job to do I
would put the correspondence in my in draw and
deal with it and then file the documentation
appropriately. 99 percent of correspondence that
comes in the mail to a legal practice is of a
confidential nature.

I also did the wages. Every week she would
approve any payments I needed to make. I had
personal fines and an attachment order was put on
my wages so this was included in the
documentation I presented to her.

Cherie never once questioned it. I had my work
hat on with dealing with this and it was not
necessary to have a conversation about this to
myself.

Cherie had come across a filed email about my
fines in one of the folders. If I was trying to hide
anything I certainly would not have filed the
documentation. It would have been shredded.
Cherie accused me of hiding things from her.

Every week she gave her code so I could complete
the wages bank transfers which included the $40
going to pay my fines. Not once did she ask me
about it. I was so nervous that she would. At the
mediation meeting this is what she got me on. My
job ended. I was unfairly dismissed.

I had no job but was a lot happier. The stress had
been lifted. People noticed the change. No job is
worth a mental breakdown over.

Poor Ian, my previous boss, the amount of times I
called him for advice and support. I was looking
for another job through this time but was not able
to find a job.

Ian told me in one phone call that I was doing the
right thing by looking for another job. Perhaps
Cherie blacklisted me. Will never know.

Cherie, looking back was not ethical in other ways.
For instance, she redid her father's will, another
lawyer friend was supposed to have prepared it but
I know she did it, had him sign it and had it
witnessed.

He was a lovely old man, I liked hearing his war stories, his time in the air force during WWII.

Cherie was from a large family and they did not get along. Cherie's father died while I was working for her and I attended his funeral.

There was also an instance where I signed a transfer document and was the temporary owner of a property and then it was transferred out of my name.

This was also questionable but I did not question Cherie, I was gullible and did as instructed. She was the boss.

Fortunately there have been no ramifications and has not come back to bite me.

After the job ended Katy and I became good friends and have compared notes and it was Katy that referred to Cherie as Psycho, which is a very fitting title. I have mentioned to Katy that I was writing about my experiences working for Cherie and her response was "sounds like a horror". I am most likely under reporting how bad the situation was.

8.   My journey as an Artist

When I moved to Dannevirke I did a search on Facebook and found out about the Dannevirke Art Society.

I went along one day and did a painting of this green bottle. It really was quite wonky.

I also heard about art classes so started to attend though had a clash with the teacher one day. I was not the only one though. Most people at some stage would clash with her. She had one of those personalities…

A friend I made at those art classes told me about another weekly class in Dannevirke – Art Made Easy.

What I liked about these classes is not only did I learn technique but also came away with completed works.

One technique I leant was what we called the credit card technique. My first exhibition was that year and I exhibited paintings using that technique. I entered into the Heather Foote Trophy competition at the Dannevirke Art Society annual exhibition. This competition was for those artists with under 4 years painting experience.

Another member of the art society told me about
The Learning Connexion. Google is your friend so
I went home with the intention of finding out
more. I could do this course by distance learning
so I enrolled with the Learning Connexion to do a
Certificate of Art and Creativity Level 4.

Then I completed a Diploma in Art and Creativity
Level 5 followed by Level 6.

Level 6 was really challenging as it had certain
criteria or boxes I had to have ticked.

One of those boxes involved setting up a Facebook
page for my art and attempting to market my art.

The tutors at The Learning Connexion were
excellent. Once I completed Level 6 I floundered
for a while as doing a course gave me direction
and goals.

I was not accepted into the Level 7 programme.

Belonging to an art society gave me the
opportunity to exhibit my work and even on
occasion have sold paintings.

Right at the end of my second Dannevirke annual
exhibition I sold 4 of my painting which was great
as I did not need to take them home with me.

With art and writing we all need to start somewhere. I have seen how my style and results have improved over time and I now have some pieces that I love and still enjoy looking at.

Others not so much. I have my favourites.

My art journey is no where near over and I keep improving all the time.

With art it is a personal thing as what one person likes or loves, another will hate.

Even if you don't like another person's style it is still possible to admire their skill and even learn from them.

# 9.	Breast Cancer

In 2021 I was diagnosed with breast cancer. I had gone for my 2 yearly mammogram and for the first time I was recalled. I got the notification that I had to go into Palmerston North for tests as they found something in one of the scans.

My partner Kevin took me in for the appointment. Now Kevin said he did not want a mention but how can I not, when he is such a huge part of my life.

Kevin was so supportive. That day, not only did I have a repeat Mammogram but also a biopsy. The biopsy showed I had cancer and that I would need surgery. It was stage 3 but caught early. A treatment plan was decided upon.

Once we got back to Dannevirke, Kevin pulled into the New World car park, went in to New World and came out with a couple of boxes of chocolates. I like chocolate. Was a nice surprise.

On the day I was booked in for surgery Kevin took me over to Palmerston North Hospital. I was to stay overnight, or so I was told, but then they were undecided.

After surgery Oxygen my levels were low and it was quite late when they eventually found me a bed for the night, in a room all to myself. It was quite a nice room.

Once settled Kevin had to return home to attend to the dogs, Theo and Maddie. They were not used to being left for so long. Monty, my horse, missed out on his feed that day. It was June, so middle of winter and he needed a daily feed as he dropped condition in winter. My miniature horses did not need feeding.

Kevin really stepped up through this time as I was not able to attend to them at all for quite some time.

Kevin would take me out to check them on the weekend so I could make sure they were looking good. More for his reassurance that he was doing a great job. He was.

After surgery I needed 3 weeks of radiation therapy but did not require chemotherapy as there would be no benefit to having chemotherapy.

The St John health shuttle was amazing. It would pick me up daily and take me to Palmy hospital and bring me home again. The drivers are all volunteers.

Going into Palmy every weekday for 3 weeks was tiring. It was my new normal during this period of time.

I got through this trying time. Not easy but it could have been far worse. I am on medication, more as a preventative measure, have yearly mammograms and check-ups with the surgical team and with the cancer GP. I am now cancer free. Life is good.

I wrote this poem below:

Diagnosis

Feeling sad
Things I cannot do
Not quite recovered
Two years on

Since surgery
Then therapy
Zapped energy
Motivations too

Though am blessed
Am still here
Was caught early
Being Stage 3.

10.   My Journey as a Writer

As a child I wanted to be a writer and now as an older adult I am now pursuing that dream. There have been times when I have dabbled but then put it aside for a time.

In 2022 I completed a creative writing course with the College of Media and Publishing. I even wrote an act to a play and a poem of which I got an A.

Quite enjoyed doing that. Since then I have written a variety of poems and have published two poetry collections. Published a children's picture book "My Nana Rhodes" and have other children's stories written but as yet unpublished.

Doing a course gives direction and helps to set personal goals and to me this is very important.

It shows one is making progress and is a real achievement when the next milestone is reached.

However, it is important to realise we have never "made it." In life we never stop learning and improving.

As well as various Facebook writing groups I now attend the Dannevike Writer's Group and the Dannevirke Poetry Group, both are held monthly at the Dannevirke Library.

Please enjoy the following segments of my writing:

a. **ACT ONE**

The curtain rises. Maggie stormed into the lounge where Sally and Heather were sitting, obviously angry as she was glaring at Sally and Heather. Sally and Heather were watching a movie and it was obvious they did not appreciate the interruption.

MAGGIE: "Someone made a complaint to WINZ about me. Who was it? Was it you Sally? Just the type of thing you would do. But why? What have I done to you to deserve this?" (*angry/loud tone of voice*).

SALLY: "Calm down. What happened? I don't know what you are talking about".

MAGGIE: "I only told you and Heather. So if it was not you then it must have been Heather."

HEATHER: "I have not spoken to anyone at WINZ. You must have told someone else."

MAGGIE: "I didn't and you know it." So which one of you two was it?"

SALLY and HEATHER: *together* "Not me."

When neither owns up Maggie storms out of the lounge, still very angry, slamming the door behind her. The curtain closes.

b. **Friendship Death**

True sadness
When a friendship ends

Moving on is hard and takes time to grieve
Years of friendship yet not real

What has one done wrong?
That the cycle has repeated

I am not always to blame
Though it sure feels like it!

The realisation that I am no longer useful.

Friends masquerading
Not real

Apology not accepted
Try to mend the fake friendship

Is it worth it, this hurt?
I miss you my friend that never was.

c. **Long Commute**

I woke up late this morning. I overslept. So late! Not this again! I jumped out of bed, heart pounding.

I dragged on some clothes, such a long commute across the hallway to work.

Turned on my computer and log on.

I need coffee!

Rush to the kitchen to turn on the jug, trying not to trip on the rubbish scattering the hallway.

A watched jug is never quick.

I made it with 20 seconds to spare. And no one was here yet for the briefing call…then I realised it was Saturday…I could have stayed in bed…

d. **Larra**

I thought I was losing my mind
I put it there, I was sure

On the table with the bread
Margarine not in the fridge, I looked

I look out the back
And there Larra was

A lovely time was being had
My mind was not lost afterall.

e. **Journal Entry**

Hi, my name is Debbie and today I bought a journal.

This is my first entry.

Often I feel so alone and that nobody really cares or even tries to listen to me. I thought a journal might be a way that I am able to not feel so alone.

People, I find, are so wrapped up in their own issues, whatever they might be and have the idea that their problems are bigger than anyone else's.

This is not right and has a way of making me feel inferior and that I do not matter.

Personally I think that no one's problems are bigger than another's, just different. But then I tend to put other people before myself and I realise this needs to stop. People as a rule are selfish.

Looking back I realise that I have been abused much in my life. Not in an obvious way, sometimes the person may not have realised what they were doing and how I was being treated was wrong.

Sometimes it was subtle abuse or manipulation. Could have been as simply bending me to their will, doing simple tasks their way.

I would be trying to fit in and often would try to adapt, even just to fit in. If I complained to a mutual friend it was always me that had the problem.

Being misunderstood comes in many forms. Caused me to feel worse about the situation so I tend to keep my thoughts and feelings in, not wanting to offend or it to come back and bite me in the proverbial.

One such example of this was when a flatmate saw how I was hanging my washing on the line and insisted I hang it the way he did. He was projecting what had once been done to him.

My way was going round the line whereas his way was to come out in sections regardless if the line was going to be needed for his washing on that particular day. That was the way I had to do it.

Seems I have been controlled by others all my life.

I don't think others have the same issues that I do. There was another instance where I was out with a group of friends and one friend took exception to a comment I made and reacted. I was hurt.

Another friend told me to "leave it". Looking back I realise she knew more about the situation the other friend was going through. She did not handle it very well as I was the rejected one and I did not know what I had done wrong.

What she should have said was that the other friend was going through something and that it was not me. I would have accepted and understood then.

I generally have always put others before myself. I am a caring person like that. A very sensitive person which is why I get hurt so easily.

Through the years I have had to learn not to let people guilt trip me. When I say no and look out for myself I am made out to be the bad person, all because they did not get what they were after.

It has been a very hard lesson to learn. Saying no does not come easy to me. Being so sensitive I get hurt and feel rejected often then that person gets on with life, without any care as to the psychological damage they have caused to another, often wiping a friendship of many years.

The painful lesson I learnt was that the friendship was not a true friendship. I know how to be a true friend but it seems many no longer have this skill. Could be the modern world we live in.

The Bible issues warnings about this sort of thing. People simply cannot be trusted unless of course there is something in it for them. This is very sad.

People are basically selfish and inward looking. Not how I was brought up to be.

f. **Christmas Myth**

Christmas
A lonely time for many
No family
Dysfunction
Same result

Lonely
Crowded room
Around the dinner table

All it takes is one
Flying arguments
Storming out

Christmas happy times
A myth.

g. **Shopping**

I have no money, but I still shop
It is a modern day addiction

Online purchases

Timu
Briscoes
Bed, Bath and Beyond

Goods I don't really need
Good prices,
Or so I think

Buy Now, Pay Later
My preference
AfterPay.

h. **Pearls**

Casting pearls before swine
Never good to do
Disputes with idiots

They will never get it
Energy not well spent
Brick wall banging

And so it goes
They will not learn
Superior they think

Ongoing mistakes
They know better

A wise person observes
Learns by observing
Changes direction
Correct choices made.

<h3 style="text-align:center">i. **Pine**</h3>

Christmas tree
Decorated with childhood memories

Big tree in the corner
Presents underneath

Tangy and sharp

That fleeting pinewood smell

Fresh
Invigorating
Slightly minty

Artificial pine
Not the same
No fragrance
Unreal.

j. **Strawberries**

Strawberries are nice
Many uses

Preserves
Jam, butter and toast

Pavlova dessert topping
Strawberries with whipped cream

Sprinkled Icing sugar
Ice cream too
Yum yum.

k. **Not Forgotten**

I forgive you
But will not forget
I will never allow you or anyone else
To hurt me that way again.

The hurt is real
The betrayal is true
I trusted you
A lesson learned
Never again.

1. **My Day**

Everyone
But Me
Is allowed to blob

Not me though
Called lazy

Even when in pain

Need to rest
Get so tired

Life gets me down

Can only cope
With small doses

Not by choice
Being this way

To do more with my day
Not sleep it away.

m. **Living
Water**

Water can hurt
Stinging

It can cleanse

For a parched throat
In the heat of the day

Water can heal

River flows troubles away
Springing life, forever new.

n. **Writer's Block**

Writer's block
What can I say?
Just writing what springs to mind!
Just to get something on the page.

Run out of ideas
What to write about
Ideas, ideas, ideas
I think has gone on holiday!

Patricia Gilmour - as a child she wanted to be an artist but felt that she couldn't draw so decided she wanted to be a writer instead. Patricia Gilmour was inspired by Enid Blyton, as one of her books started her love of reading.

Art remained her favourite school subject, though this was not pursued until as an older adult when she joined the Dannevirke Art Society and completed a Diploma in Art and Creativity Level 6 with The Learning Connexion.

Patricia Gilmour has also completed various writing courses to pursue her second childhood dream.

Like and follow her Facebook page - Patricia Gilmour – Artist and Writer

https://www.facebook.com/profile.php?id=100039556099601

www.ingramcontent.com/pod-product-compliance
Lightning Source LLC
Chambersburg PA
CBHW050008040726
47599CB00014B/1277